4

W9-ANI-566

Freedom
of Speech

Freedom of Speech

J. Edward Evans

 Lerner Publications Company · Minneapolis

Front cover photo by Lori Waselchuk

Cover illustration by George Overlie

Library of Congress Cataloging-in-Publication Data

Evans, J. Edward.
    Freedom of speech / J. Edward Evans.
        p.   cm.
    Includes bibliographical references.
    Summary: Traces the history of the concept of freedom of speech,
discusses how the Supreme Court has interpreted the constitutional
amendment, and provides historical and present-day examples of why
the issue is controversial.
    ISBN 0-8225-1753-1 (lib. bdg.)
    1. Freedom of speech—United States—Juvenile literature.
2. Freedom of speech—United States—History—Juvenile literature.
[1. Freedom of speech. 2. Freedom of speech—History.] I. Title.
KF4772.Z9E94   1990
342.73'0853—dc20
[347.302853]   89-13730
                                                              CIP
                                                               AC

Manufactured in the United States of America

1 2 3 4 5 6 7 8 9 10 99 98 97 96 95 94 93 92 91 90

Contents

Citizens of the United States can speak to groups about nearly any topic without worrying that they will be arrested. Freedom of speech also means people can express their ideas in other ways as well. Many people publish pamphlets to express their views on certain topics.

1
Free Speech: Freedom to Express Ideas

People in the United States of America take pride in living in a country that is known as the land of liberty. As citizens, we believe we have certain rights as individuals. We also believe these rights cannot be taken away by anyone, for any reason.

Among these rights is freedom of speech. We usually think of speech just as spoken words. But freedom of speech means much more than merely allowing people to say whatever they want whenever they feel like it. It means having the freedom to express ideas. It means having the freedom to believe what you choose and to openly state your beliefs without fear of being thrown in jail.

Freedom of speech is so closely tied to freedom of ideas that the authors of the United States Constitution could not separate the two. The First Amendment to the Constitution covers a number of freedoms—including freedom of religion and press—that have one thing in common. Each of them guarantees that United States citizens have the right to hold and express their ideas, regardless of how government officials feel about those ideas. The First Amendment states:

Congress shall make no law restricting an establishment of religion, or prohibiting the free exercise thereof; or abridging the freedom of speech, or of the press; or the rights of the people peaceably to assemble, and to petition the Government for a redress of grievances.

The writers of the First Amendment believed that freedom of ideas was crucial in order for a democracy to survive. A government of the people had to allow its citizens the right to disagree with actions of government officials. A democracy had to allow candidates for public office the right to explain their views. If citizens were not allowed to speak their minds on all subjects, then the government would no longer be the people's government.

This book will focus on the simplest and most direct forms of free speech activity. Conversation, speeches, pamphlets, and carrying protest signs are all ways of presenting ideas. They can be carried out by individuals acting alone or together. Because these forms of communication require little or no money to produce, they are open to everyone.

Different Interpretations

It is easy to think of a law as something that is clear and obvious. Certain actions are allowed by law, other actions are not allowed by law. But the difference between legal and illegal actions is not always so distinct. In fact, there is often a great deal of argument over what a law means or does not mean. This is especially true of the issue of freedom of speech.

Some people believe that when the First Amendment says that Congress shall make no law abridging freedom of speech, that is exactly what it means. "No law means no law," wrote longtime Supreme Court Justice Hugo Black. Justice Black

Supreme Court Justice Hugo Black believed in absolute freedom of speech. He thought there should be no laws restricting speech whatsoever.

Congress proposed 12 amendments, or additions, to the Constitution. The states approved 10 of the 12, and the articles became known as the Bill of Rights. The Bill of Rights is reprinted in an appendix that begins on page 66 of this book.

believed that free speech is so important to a democracy that nothing should be allowed to interfere with it. People must be allowed to believe and express even those opinions with which many others disagree. Any attempt by the government to restrict a person's freedom of expression opens the way to destroying that freedom for all of us. For our own protection, the government must not be allowed to decide which ideas are acceptable.

Other people disagree. They argue that the First Amendment was not intended to leave government helpless to act against people whose speech can cause great harm to other United States citizens. Legislators have sometimes taken this view. Despite the wording of the First Amendment, Congress has passed laws limiting freedom of speech.

Total freedom of speech can lead to situations that make even the most freedom-loving American uncomfortable. Should people be able to make speeches calling for a violent attack on government? Should a person be allowed to use a public place to preach hatred against blacks, Jews, Catholics, or any other race or religion that he or she happens to dislike? Is it all right for someone to say out loud in a public place that the president of the United States should be shot? Should a person be allowed to threaten to hurt another person?

Does freedom of speech allow a person to joke about having a gun in his or her pocket while boarding an airplane? Should two groups that are bitterly opposed to each others' ideas be allowed to demonstrate in the same place, when it is likely that fights or a riot could break out? Should there be any restrictions on obscene or swear words or on terrible insults? Does freedom of speech give someone the right to tell lies about another person?

How much freedom is too much? Because of questions like these, many people believe that there must be restrictions on freedom of speech. But few people agree on exactly what those restrictions should be.

It is the task of the judges in the United States court system to make those distinctions. Charles Evans Hughes, chief justice of the United States from 1930 to 1941, once explained the role of judges in deciding how much freedom people have. He said that although the country is governed by a constitution, "the Constitution is what the judges say it is." However, even the judges of the Supreme Court frequently hold

Chief Justice Charles Evans Hughes said that one of the Supreme Court's roles is to decide whether or not certain laws or activities are allowed by the Constitution.

opposite views on many freedom of speech issues.

Freedom of speech has meant different things at different times in United States history. One of the reasons for different interpretations is that judges are influenced by attitudes of society and by the will of the people. History has shown that **public opinion** has a strong influence on how much or how little freedom of speech is allowed in the United States. Public opinion refers to how a majority of people feel about an issue at a particular time. It changes with time.

When a Supreme Court judge retires, the president appoints a new judge to the bench. Each judge brings his or her own ideas and opinions to the Supreme Court and votes according to those beliefs. Many issues that come before the Supreme Court are decided by slim margins. Occasionally, one vote is enough to shift the Court's majority opinion from one side of an issue to the other.

How much freedom do you think should be allowed? Your answer and the answers of your fellow citizens will shape the future of this country.

In order to answer responsibly, we all must study the issue carefully. Three things can help us decide how free we want speech to be: 1) understanding the past; 2) knowing the arguments in favor of widespread freedom of speech and the arguments for limiting such freedom; and 3) thinking about how much freedom of speech will make the United States the kind of nation we want it to be.

Before the United States was founded, few countries allowed their citizens the freedom to speak out on governmental issues.

2
An Old Value or a New Idea?

Freedom of speech is a United States tradition that is as old as the nation itself. Many of the ideas about freedom that the founders of the United States used in building our government have been around far longer than the United States. The founders borrowed ideas from great thinkers who lived centuries before them.

Yet when compared to the long span of world history, the freedom of people to criticize their governments is a relatively new notion. Historically, conditions have seldom been right for widespread acceptance of the idea of free speech. The ideas put into practice by United States founders more than 200 years ago were a radical challenge to the accepted power of governments. This bold experiment with freedom did not end when the First Amendment was written.

Over time, the definition of freedom of speech has broadened and changed, and the changes have occurred at an ever-faster rate. In the last half century, U.S. citizens have enjoyed far greater freedom of speech than existed when the First Amendment was adopted. Legal historians say almost all of the country's court rulings that shape freedom of speech have taken place in the last 70 years.

Freedom of speech is an old idea that has its roots in ancient Western civilization. In order to understand freedom of speech, we first need to examine those roots.

Silence for the Good of Society

The citizens of ancient Athens were known for their love of freedom. But their belief in freedom was put to a severe test by the great philosopher, Socrates. Socrates frequently tried to find out why people thought and acted the way they did. His frequent, sometimes critical, questioning made many Athenians angry.

Socrates was executed in Athens by people who were upset with his teaching methods and his religious views, which were different from their own.

These people could not silence Socrates simply for criticizing them. But they found another way to limit his freedom of speech. They accused Socrates of corrupting the youth of the city and also of insulting the gods. Almost all cultures have held that these two actions are crimes—each society tries to protect its children and its sacred beliefs. Socrates's enemies considered his trial a battle that tested which was more important—individual freedom or preservation of society's **values**. Values are things—such as honesty, family life, and kindness—that people consider to be important.

Society's values won. Socrates said he never intended to offend the gods or corrupt children. He insisted that he was only seeking the truth. The people of Athens paid no heed to Socrates's arguments, and he was condemned to death. Socrates had chances to escape, but he was determined to sacrifice his life for the right to speak freely. He died after drinking a cup of poisonous hemlock in the ancient Greek method of execution.

History offers countless other examples of people who suffered for criticizing authorities. The arguments used against them were often

Galileo appears before officials of the Roman Catholic Church. After scientific studies of the planetary system, Galileo declared his belief that the Earth revolved around the sun. As a member of the Roman Catholic Church, he was forced to withdraw his statement because it was the opposite of a theory taught by the church.

the same: that criticism of the government, its laws, or its leaders weakens the government. Anything that threatened the government also threatened society, and therefore must not be allowed.

Religious leaders often used the same reason. They said criticism of religious leaders or of positions taken by the church weakened the religious group and could not be tolerated. As a result, brilliant thinkers such as the Italian astronomer, Galileo, were silenced. Galileo taught that the Earth was not the center of the universe, but that it rotated around the sun. Leaders of the Roman Catholic Church said the Earth indeed was at the center and that the sun revolved around it. They forced Galileo to deny his own beliefs.

Bloody persecution of those who differed with authorities on religious matters was common in Europe for centuries. Those who differed with authorities on government matters could expect cruel treatment as well. By suppressing opinions that were different from their own, society's leaders were free to perform their duties without opposition. In exchange for this strength of society, individuals gave up their freedom of ideas.

Even people who were loyal to their country, however, realized that some arguments against allowing freedom of speech were misleading. Many government rulers were tyrants. By forbidding criticism of themselves, these rulers ensured that they could impose their wishes—no matter how fair or unfair—on society. That was hardly a good way to keep a society strong!

The English Influence

Efforts of people to gain the right to free speech have taken place in many countries over the centuries. The authors of the United States Constitution, who had been ruled by English royalty, were most familiar with those efforts in England.

Perhaps the most important breakthrough for individual rights occurred in 1215. In that year, King John of England was under great pressure to grant certain rights to the English nobility, who were upset with his abuses of power. In order to head off an almost-certain rebellion, King John signed the Magna Carta. In the document, he agreed that his noble servants had certain rights and that it was not the privilege of a king to do whatever he chose without regard for those rights.

King John of England abused his powers as king. When a group of barons raised an army to revolt against him, King John was forced to sign the Magna Carta.

In 1352 the British **Parliament**, the governing body, passed a law that limited the types of actions that could be considered **treason**. (Treason is a betrayal of or disloyalty to a ruler or country.) It, too, was an important step in recognizing that there was a need for more individual rights. But neither this law nor the Magna Carta gave people a great deal of free speech liberties. For instance, under the Magna Carta, the government could still inflict severe punishment for anyone who criticized the royal family or even so much as "imagined the death of the king."

Persons who expressed their criticisms of government figures did so at their own risk well into the 17th century. In 1579, for example, John Stubbs launched his public opposition to the proposed marriage of Queen Elizabeth I to a Frenchman. Such criticism was illegal and Stubbs's right hand was cut off as

punishment. The government went so far as to put Stubbs's lawyer in jail for daring to represent him at the trial.

During the reign of Charles I, in 1636, William Prynne published a book that was very critical of the theater. Because King Charles I enjoyed the theater and the queen herself was an amateur actress, the book was considered to be an attack on the king. Prynne was sentenced to life imprisonment, and his ears were cut off.

It was not only the "common" people who had to keep their thoughts to themselves; even members of Parliament were not permitted to debate the issues on which they were to vote. When Queen Elizabeth was asked in 1593 to allow debate on the floor of Parliament, she replied, "Privilege of speech is granted, but you must know what privilege you have; not to speak every one what he listeth, or what cometh in his brain to utter that; but your privilege is Aye or No." In other words, the queen believed that their freedom

In the 17th century, when King Charles I (left) ruled, people were still given harsh punishment for saying or writing things that were thought to be critical of the royal family and government.

17

of speech consisted only of the right to vote on the legislation, not to discuss it.

Parliament had no better luck arguing its case before King James I, who succeeded Elizabeth as ruler of England. James issued a proclamation against "excess of lavish and licentious speech on matters of state." According to the king, matters of state were "no theames, or subjects fit for vulgar persons, or common meetings. . . ." He ordered anyone who heard an English citizen discussing public affairs to report that person within 24 hours or be sent to prison. So strong were his feelings about citizens speaking out on public affairs that he considered anyone who neglected to report such a crime to be as guilty as the person committing it.

Despite the repeated protests of its members, Parliament did not win the freedom to debate issues until 1689. However, the right was but a small step in the direction of liberty. Freedom of speech was only for Parliament, which was merely a branch of the government. In practice, the new rule still allowed only government members to speak on government matters. Even as Parliament was fighting for its own right to free speech, it supported stiff penalties for the common people who dared to speak their minds on public issues.

The Underground Presses

People with ideas are always looking for ways to share their ideas with others. The development of printing presses gave the common people a powerful tool for making their opinions known.

Authorities had suspected from the beginning that the printing press could cause problems for them. Shortly after printing presses with movable type came into widespread use in the late 15th century, society's leaders worked to control the press. By the early 16th century, both government and church officials had imposed **censorship**. (Censorship refers to the act of withholding, confiscating, or deleting material so it cannot be printed, broadcast, or distributed.) They ruled that nothing could be printed unless it was licensed. In order to get **licenses**, printers had to have the material approved beforehand by an official reader, or censor. Licenses gave printers official permission to print. Of course, nothing which contained criticism of the government or church would be licensed. Authorities used

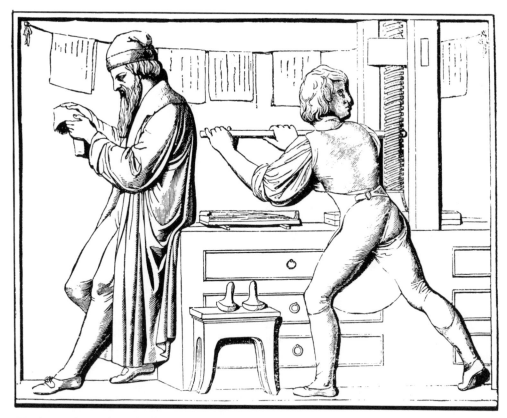

The invention of a printing press with movable type gave people more opportunities to express their ideas. Before then, printing many copies of a document or pamphlet was a long and tedious process.

this method of censorship to limit freedom of speech until the end of the 17th century.

The censorship was not completely successful, however. People, sometimes using made-up names or no names at all, wrote pamphlets on a variety of topics, including religion and politics. Rather than submitting these pamphlets to the censors, they published them without permission. The press operators sometimes risked severe punishment, as did the authors of these pamphlets. But enough people were committed to freedom of speech that 17th-century England was flooded with unlicensed pamphlets.

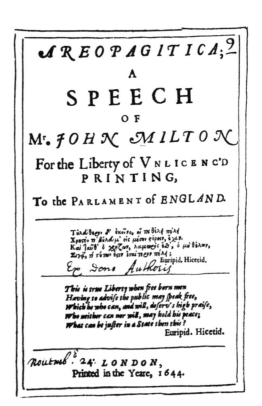

AREOPAGITICA; A SPEECH OF Mr. JOHN MILTON For the Liberty of VNLICENC'D PRINTING, To the PARLAMENT of ENGLAND.

This is true Liberty when free born men
Having to advise the public may speak free,
Which he who can, and will, deserv's high praise,
Who neither can nor will, may hold his peace;
What can be juster in a State then this?
Euripid. Hicetid.

LONDON,
Printed in the Yeare, 1644.

The English poet John Milton wrote a pamphlet, Areopagitica, *in which he urged Parliament to give people the right to publish pamphlets and other materials without licenses.*

This daring exchange of ideas attracted far greater audiences than the standard, government-approved pamphlets. Crowds frequently gathered to discuss the ideas printed in the latest unlicensed pamphlet. An increasing number of men and women learned how to read so they could participate in the lively discussions.

A number of these pamphlets were written by John Milton, one of the most respected poets in the history of English literature. In 1644 he put out a pamphlet in which he called for an end to restrictions on printing. Milton argued that the licensing system prevented people from learning the truth as much as it kept them from hearing lies. He explained that people accept ideas to which they are accustomed without really thinking about them.

What happens then, he asked, when someone presents a new idea that makes a traditional way of thinking seem false? The natural reaction is to think that it is the new idea which is false.

> . . . If it comes to prohibiting, there is not aught more likely to be prohibited than truth itself; whose first appearance to our eyes bleared and dimmed with prejudice and custom is more unsightly and unplausible than many errors . . .

Milton wrote that there was no reason to be afraid of false ideas. He was convinced that when both true and false statements were heard, truth would win out. The only result of censorship, then, was to prevent the spread of true ideas.

Like Socrates, Milton found that

The trial of John Peter Zenger. Government officials sought to control printing in the colonies well into the 18th century. Newspaper publishers were frequently accused of seditious libel and brought to trial for criticizing the English government officials who ruled the colonies.

his ideas on freedom of speech were too radical for many people to accept. Although his pamphlets are often quoted today, Milton's arguments had little influence on public policy. Licensing of printing continued for another half century in England. In colonial America, printing was strictly controlled long after the English licensing law was removed.

The Truth Hurts

Again, the end of the censorship laws in the last years of the 17th century did not lead to freedom of speech as it would come to be known in the 20th century. It only delayed the punishment given to those who exercised their free speech. True, no one could tell a person beforehand what he or she could say or write. But after the speech was made or the words printed, government could hand out harsh punishments if it did not approve of what was said or printed. Under the law of **seditious libel**, it was a crime to print or say anything intended to hurt the good standing of the king or government. As late as the 18th century, people were imprisoned, fined, and whipped for what we consider to be ordinary political discussion.

Criticism of the government was

The colonists, led by George Washington, fought the American Revolution to escape what they felt was unfair treatment. They disliked restrictions on their speech, taxes on goods brought into the country, and other restrictions of their freedom.

regarded as an attack against the government, and could not be allowed. Criticism that was true was far more damaging to the government than false criticism. For that reason, accurate criticism was sometimes considered a greater crime than careless **slander**. (Speech that is false and harmful to someone's reputation is called slander.)

At the time of the American Revolution, there was still no guarantee of free speech for English subjects. In colonial America, in fact, local governments were often harder on their critics than were representatives of the English government.

3
Free Speech in the New Country

With the American Revolution, which was fought from 1775 to 1783, the United States won independence from England. The colonists were free to set up whatever form of government they desired. Many of them had fought the war because they felt they had been treated unfairly by the English. They only wanted their new nation to give them the same rights that the English subjects living in England enjoyed.

Others, such as Thomas Jefferson and James Madison, wanted more. They saw the creation of their new nation as a rare opportunity to secure rights that had been denied even to English citizens. For example, under English law it was still a crime for people to criticize the government.

Madison thought the English government had far too much power because of laws that discouraged the free exchange of ideas.

Knowing that governments all through history had limited the freedoms of its citizens, leaders such as Madison and Jefferson were determined to protect people in the new country from government. In the Declaration of Independence, Jefferson wrote on behalf of the Continental Congress that there were many rights over which governments should have no control:

We hold these truths to be self-evident, that all men are created equal, that they are endowed by their Creator with certain unalienable Rights; that among these are Life, Liberty and the pursuit of Happiness.— That to secure these rights, Governments are instituted among Men, deriving their just powers from the consent of the governed, ...

In others words, the Declaration said people did not exist for the benefit of governments. Rather, governments existed for the benefit of people. Liberty and justice were not privileges that could be granted or denied by a government; they were rights that a government should be sworn to protect at all costs.

The Declaration of Independence described the ideals on which the government of the United States was built. The Constitution, written in 1787, set up the rules under which the government would operate. Much of the Constitution was influenced by the ideals presented in the Declaration of Independence. Members of the Constitutional Convention agreed that a government that was truly the servant of the people must allow its citizens to believe what they choose and to say what they believe. They eliminated much of the threat of treason that

George Washington speaks to delegates at the Constitutional Convention in Philadelphia, Pennsylvania. The delegates wanted to make sure that the new country's federal government respected the common person's rights.

stifled free speech. Of all the acts considered to be treason, outlined by the English Parliament in 1352, delegates to the Constitutional Convention kept only two: waging war against the country, and "adhering to" its enemies.

Leaders of several states, however, believed that the Constitution did not go far enough to protect citizens from the abuses of government power. They refused to ratify, or approve, the document because it did not clearly spell out the basic rights and liberties which the government could not take away. The Constitution was ratified by most of the states by June 1788, but only after plans were made to amend it immediately to list these rights.

The Bill of Rights

One of the first duties of the United States Congress was to decide what amendments to include in this "Bill of Rights." Hundreds of ideas were introduced. In the end, the House of Representatives settled on 17 proposed amendments, which were written by James Madison. The United States Senate reduced that number to 12 by combining several of the amendments. Those 12 amendments were sent to the states for ratification.

In order for the amendments to become part of the Constitution, three-fourths of the states had to agree to them. On December 15, 1791, Virginia became the 10th state to approve 10 of the 12 amendments, thereby making those 10 into law. These amendments, called the Bill of Rights, provided United States citizens with more guarantees of freedom than any government had ever granted before. Among these was the First Amendment.

What Exactly Does Free Speech Mean?

The statement "Congress shall make no law . . . abridging the freedom of speech" was widely accepted. It was clear that the freedom to hold and express beliefs was crucial to a government of free people. The First Amendment seemed to be a straightforward guarantee of that important freedom. While other amendments were debated, there were no arguments about free speech.

Only seven years after the First Amendment was adopted, however, Americans discovered that it was not as clear-cut as they had thought. During a bitter division between the two main political parties of the time, people began to question

25

Thomas Jefferson (left) and James Madison (right) fought to preserve freedom of speech, even if it meant government would be criticized. Both men eventually served terms as president.

whether freedom of speech was a practical idea. The Federalists, led by Alexander Hamilton and John Adams, held ideas about government that were different from those held by the Republicans, led by Jefferson and Madison.

According to the election rules of the time, the presidential candidate receiving the second-highest total of votes in the election became vice president. That left President John Adams, a Federalist, with a Republican, Thomas Jefferson, as his vice president. Although the two were supposed to be working together to head the government, they were actually working against each other on many issues. Before long, the battles between the two factions became fierce.

The split between the parties

Alexander Hamilton (left) and John Adams (right) wanted to restrict speech so government would not have to put up with what they felt was irresponsible criticism.

widened in 1798 when the United States was fighting an undeclared war against France. Federalists accused the Republicans of siding with the French. Jefferson's supporters, with an eye on the 1800 election, fought back with speeches and articles that viciously attacked Adams and the Federalists.

Federalists found some of the criticism so offensive that they asked themselves what the First Amendment really meant. Did free speech mean that government leaders had to put up with irresponsible public abuse? Did it give people the right to tell lies about government officials? When the intent of the speech was to damage the government, couldn't that qualify as treason? The Federalists eventually introduced the Alien and Sedition Acts of 1798.

Sounding much like the old English law of seditious libel, the Sedition Act made it a crime to write, print, or speak any false, scandalous, and malicious criticism of the president, Congress, or government of the United States, if the intention was to harm their reputations or "to incite against them the hatred of the good people of the United States."

Suddenly the debates that were missing in the early part of the decade, when the First Amendment was passed, began to rage. Republicans raised a cry of protest. It was from a fear of such laws that the Bill of Rights had been written. Now the Federalists were acting as if the Bill of Rights did not exist. Didn't the First Amendment prohibit *any* laws restricting freedom of speech?

The Federalists answered that the First Amendment applied to truthful, responsible speech, and reasonable differences of opinion. The Sedition Act would not affect those expressions. It contained no suggestion of censorship or prior approval of any speech. The Sedition Act only punished false, scandalous, and malicious criticisms. That kind of irresponsible speech had no place in a civilized society, the Federalists said.

But the Republicans were unswayed. Who would decide which speech is false or malicious? The law gave that power to the government, and the government would always rule that offensive criticism of it is false. How could people possibly prove otherwise in a court of law? After all, opinions are not things that can be proven true. The Sedition Act would bring an end to all political discussion, the Republicans said. People would be afraid to speak or write what they believed to be true.

The Federalists, however, controlled the majority in Congress, and they were able to pass the act. Thomas Jefferson and James Madison drafted resolutions of protest.

Their resolutions denounced the Sedition Act for exercising:

> . . . a power not delegated by the Constitution, but, on the contrary, expressly and positively forbidden by one of the amendments thereto—a power which, more than any other, ought to produce universal alarm, because it is levelled against the right of freely examining public characters and measures, and of free communication among the people thereon, which has ever been justly deemed the only effectual guardian of every other right.

Despite the Republican arguments, the government began to

28

prosecute citizens for "false" speech. Congressman Matthew Lyon of Vermont was the first person jailed under the Sedition Act. For accusing President Adams of pomp and greed, Lyon was fined $1,000 and sentenced to four months in jail. Two dozen others, all active Republicans, were arrested, and 10 of them were sentenced to jail. The effects of the Sedition Act were short-lived, however. Jefferson defeated Adams in the 1800 presidential election. President Jefferson moved swiftly to pardon those convicted under the Sedition Act. Although the Federalists still controlled Congress, no attempt was made to renew the law when it expired in 1801. In fact, Congress eventually ordered all fines paid under the law to be returned.

During Jefferson's presidency, his administration became an example of the powerful, suppressive government he distrusted. For many years Jefferson had been one of the country's most outspoken champions of free speech. In his first inaugural address, he went so far as to say that if anyone wanted to dissolve the government of the United States, or change its form, he or she could speak freely. Yet once Jefferson became the head of the government, his administration tried to subdue

Supreme Court Justice Samuel Chase was brought to trial for things he said about the government during Jefferson's presidency.

his critics. Rather than going against the First Amendment, however, the advisers found a way around it. At the time, the First Amendment applied only to federal laws, so Jefferson's advisers used state **libel** laws to silence his opposition. Libel is a false, written attack on a person's character that is intended to harm that person's reputation.

In 1804 Supreme Court Justice Samuel Chase, a Federalist who had signed the Declaration of

The Battle of New Orleans during the War of 1812, between the United States and Great Britain. Even when people worked against the war, President James Madison refused to place any restrictions on freedom of speech.

Independence, was accused of making libelous and seditious statements about Jefferson's administration. He was impeached and tried by the Senate but was acquitted, or found innocent, of the charges.

James Madison, who succeeded Jefferson as president, never wavered in his devotion to free speech. During the War of 1812, a political party in New England spoke out and worked against the United States war effort. Although he was under heavy pressure from supporters who feared that such opposition would destroy the country, Madison refused to silence those critics. Not even scandalous attacks on his own reputation could move Madison to interfere with the right of free speech.

The passage of the Sedition Act and the debates over free speech that followed in the Jefferson and Madison administrations forced U.S. citizens to think more carefully about the effects of free speech. These experiences verified the idea that free people had to be very cautious about the limits they set on the right to hold and express opinions. If they were not careful, individual rights could be eroded very quickly. The United States public wanted the broadest possible freedom to criticize the government, public officials, and candidates for office.

Free Speech in Times of War

For the next one hundred years following Madison's term, there seemed to be a general public consensus, or agreement, on what freedom of speech meant. During that time, not a single case involving freedom of speech was appealed to the Supreme Court. For the most part, the government was not involved in freedom of speech issues.

Wartime restrictions on speech eventually reopened the public debate on freedom of speech. People

President Abraham Lincoln talks with General George McClellan, right, near a battlefield during the Civil War. Even though there were instances in which constitutional rights were violated, U.S. citizens experienced few restrictions on their freedom.

felt the benefits of free speech had to be balanced against situations in which many lives were at stake. Serious opposition to government acts during wartime could put the lives of soldiers, and even the future of the nation itself, in grave danger.

Prior to 1917, the United States government had no official policy on free speech during wartime. During the Civil War in the 1860s, the government restricted some of the usual freedoms. Some people who opposed government policies were arrested without charge and others were jailed for conspiring to overthrow the government. President Abraham Lincoln even ignored a court order to release some suspected traitors. Yet, at the time, none of this caused a great controversy.

Considering that the country was being torn apart by fighting between its own citizens, the amount of freedom allowed to political opponents was astounding. Instead of imposing martial law, as many countries often do during civil wars, the United States held open elections as scheduled. Candidates for office were free to criticize each other and the government.

But the next major war involving the United States caused a far greater strain on individual freedoms. When the United States entered World War I in 1917, government set policies that triggered a new debate on freedom of speech. The debate continued throughout the 20th century.

In order to secure more military

Once the United States began fighting in World War I, government passed laws that restricted people's freedom to criticize anything remotely associated with the war effort.

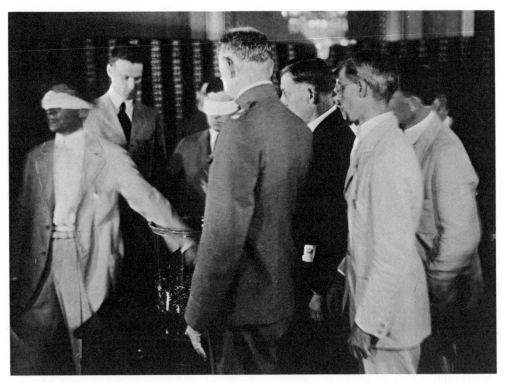

The Selective Service System, in which men were compelled to join the army when their numbers were drawn from a container, was very controversial.

personnel to fight against Germany and its allies, Congress established the Selective Service System. Commonly known as the draft, the system required young men to join the armed forces if they were called, whether they wanted to join or not. Most people thought the draft was necessary and fair. But others opposed to the war protested against the draft. Congress feared that enemies of the United States might organize a plan to disrupt the draft, which could have crippled the armed forces and caused the country to lose the war. Faced with such a possibility, Congress decided it would be better to limit freedom of speech, just a little. In 1917 Congress passed the Espionage Act. Under the Espionage Act, it was a crime to make false reports or statements that were meant to interfere with the war effort. It was a crime to persuade people to become disloyal or to persuade people not to join the armed services. It was also illegal to obstruct recruiting or enlistment.

Some people, including the attorney general of the United States, thought that the Espionage Act did not go far enough. They believed that all citizens should support their leaders during wartime. They thought people who said the United States was wrong to fight in the war were disloyal; and that such disloyalty was dangerous to the country and should be punished.

Influenced by these arguments, Congress passed the Sedition Act of 1918. This act made it a crime, during wartime, to say, print, write, or publish anything disloyal, profane, or abusive about the U.S. government, the flag, or military uniforms. Anything that was said or done in support of any country at war against the United States was punishable by law. It was even a crime to give financial advice that was intended to obstruct the sale of United States war bonds.

Because loyalty to one's country was such an important issue at the time, many people supported these restrictions on their freedom of speech. More than 2,000 people who were prosecuted under the Sedition Act were convicted and sentenced to jail by juries made up of their fellow citizens. A number of state legislatures showed support for the Sedition Act by passing espionage and sedition acts of their own.

But it soon became apparent that even the most well-intentioned restriction of free speech can lead to trouble. The Sedition Act outlawed only those words that were spoken and written with the intention of hurting the war effort. Yet prosecutors argued that any criticism of the government was made with the intention of harming a particular aim of the government, and anything that harmed the government's aims harmed the war effort.

As a result, people were jailed for saying things that would scarcely be noticed years later. One man was arrested for saying that the country should raise taxes instead of selling war bonds. In Minnesota, police arrested a man for telling a group of women that no soldier would ever see the socks they were knitting. Criticism of the Red Cross or YMCA, groups that provided assistance to soldiers, led to arrest. Anyone discussing the war in any public place—a hotel lobby, a restaurant, a train, a park—could be arrested for using language that another

Under the Sedition Act, people criticizing the Red Cross—which set up canteens, or refreshment counters, for soldiers—could be punished.

person considered disloyal. A farmer was even arrested for something he said in his own home. He was turned in by two strangers who had come to his house for help when their car ran out of gas.

As the number of arrests increased, more people grew uncomfortable with the Sedition Act. The issue of free speech, which had lain dormant for a century, began to generate spirited debate. Most people thought that society needed some regulations, such as the Sedition Act, on free speech. Yet many people believed that a large number of the arrests made under this act were in violation of the First Amendment. The question that frightened them was this: If Congress could disregard any one part of the Bill of Rights, what would stop them from disregarding all of it? For protection, the public turned to the branch of government that had the final say on legal matters—the judicial branch. Beginning in 1919, the struggle for freedom of speech was fought in the courts.

The Supreme Court Building in Washington, D.C.

4
The Supreme Court Steps In

The Supreme Court is made up of nine members, a chief justice and eight associate justices. Supreme Court justices are appointed by the president, but the appointees must be approved by Congress before they can take office. Once they have been approved, these justices serve for as long as they are willing and able to carry out their duties.

As the highest court in the United States, the Supreme Court has the final say as to: 1) what the Constitution—the supreme law of the land—means, and 2) whether or not laws passed by Congress are allowed by the Constitution. Thomas Jefferson referred to the courts as the guardians of the rights of United States citizens. The Supreme Court is the last line of defense for preserving constitutional rights.

The Supreme Court usually does not initiate any action. Instead, it considers appeals of cases which have been decided in state or lower federal courts. On the average, about 5,000 cases decided in state courts or lower federal courts are appealed to the Supreme Court each year. The Supreme Court then chooses which of those cases it will consider. A typical workload for the Supreme Court is roughly 150 to 180 cases per year.

The questions posed to the justices are rarely simple ones to answer. Some legal experts insist that matters of constitutional law must be based on the "original intent" of the writers of the Constitution. Yet those writers could not have imagined many of the issues that would face the Court two centuries later. One of the most important framers of the Constitution, James Madison, believed the document should be read as it was without regard for the writers' intention. In fact, it was for that reason that he refused to permit the notes he made while working on the Constitution to be published during his lifetime. Others, such as Justice Thurgood Marshall, go so far as to say that the Constitution

Supreme Court Justice Thurgood Marshall says the Constitution has needed to change along with society.

was defective from the start. For instance, they point out, it did not grant any rights to black slaves or Native Americans, nor many rights to women. The argument of Marshall and others is that the Constitution is a "living document" that has needed changes over the years to give U.S. citizens the level of freedom they want. With such widespread disagreement on the basic issues, it is not surprising that, more often than not, the justices disagree in their verdicts.

After discussing the facts of a case, Supreme Court justices reach a decision through a vote. Justices can vote to overturn the lower court's decision or to agree with it. A number of important cases have been decided on 5-to-4 votes. Once a decision is reached, one of the justices in the majority writes an opinion explaining the reasoning in support of the decision. Justices who disagree with the majority then may write minority, or dissenting, opinions in which they explain why they believe the verdict was incorrect. (A **majority opinion** outlines the reasons judges voted in favor of a decision. A **minority opinion** outlines reasons why judges voted against a decision.) While their statements do not alter the decision of the

The Constitution did not grant voting rights to women. However, the Constitution allows changes to be made through amendments. The women's suffrage movement was able to push through the 19th Amendment, which guaranteed women the right to vote. Amendments allow the government to make up for shortcomings in the Constitution.

majority, dissenting opinions sometimes have important effects. Minority opinions are sometimes expressed so well that they influence the thinking of others. As new justices replace old ones, the Court may hear a case that deals with the same issue again. If a number of the new justices are persuaded by a minority opinion from a previous decision, then the former minority opinion may become the majority, and the law is changed. Any of the justices may write statements of their own about each case.

Through the years, Supreme Court opinions have helped the people of the United States to understand free speech. As even the justices themselves admit, the Court has often been wrong in its decisions and has had to correct those errors in later years. But right or wrong, justices have given clear, thoughtful reasons for limiting—or refusing to limit—speech in particular cases.

Before 1919 court cases involving freedom of speech were rare. As a result, the Supreme Court scarcely influenced the debate over free speech. But many people convicted under the Sedition Act of 1918 believed that their constitutional rights had been violated. They appealed their cases to higher courts. In 1919 the first of these cases reached the Supreme Court.

Charles Schenck claimed that the draft was not allowed by the Constitution. His belief was so strong that he passed out pamphlets, in which he wrote that anyone who submitted to the draft was "little better than a convict." In the pamphlet he urged men to resist the draft by any legal means possible. Schenck was prosecuted under the Sedition Act and found guilty of trying to cause disobedience in the armed forces and of attempting to interfere with army recruiting. Arguing that his First Amendment rights had been violated, Schenck appealed to the Supreme Court to overturn his conviction.

It was the Court's task to produce a clear answer to an ancient question: How important are the rights of individuals when compared to the

Supreme Court Justice Oliver Wendell Holmes, Jr., influenced the way other justices have felt about freedom of speech.

security of the nation? After hearing the arguments of both sides, the Court ruled that, in this case, the security of the nation was more important. In upholding Schenck's conviction, the Court declared that there are exceptions to the right to free speech.

Oliver Wendell Holmes, Jr., writing the opinion for the majority, pointed out that freedom of speech does not give a person the right to falsely shout "fire" in a crowded theater and cause panic. Wartime, he wrote, was another situation in which free speech needed to be limited for the sake of the country. In the words of Justice Holmes:

We admit that in many places and in ordinary times the [defendant] in saying all that was said in the circular [pamphlet] would have been within [his] constitutional rights. But the character of every act depends upon the circumstances in which it is done.

Referring to speech in wartime, the Court's opinion stated:

When a nation is at war many things that might be said in time of peace [hurt the war effort so much that they cannot] be endured so long as men fight ... no Court could regard them as protected by any constitutional right.

Having declared that there were exceptions to the right of free speech, the Court then had to specify what

The 1919 Supreme Court heard the first of the cases arising from the Sedition Act of 1918.

those exceptions were. It seemed that the best way to do that was to develop tests. Those actions that fulfilled all the conditions of the test would be judged to be illegal. Justice Holmes proposed one such test in his opinion on the Schenck case.

(The) question in every case is whether the words are used in such circumstances and are of such a nature as to create a clear and present danger that they will bring about the substantive evils [harm] that Congress has a right to prevent.

The Court agreed that Schenck's

Supreme Court Justice Louis Brandeis joined with Justice Holmes in developing guidelines that would prevent unnecessary restrictions of speech.

speech presented a "clear and present" danger to the country. Since none of the justices disagreed, there seemed little room for further argument. In wartime, at least, it seemed clear that the government could suspend freedoms that had been guaranteed by the Bill of Rights.

But the issue was far from settled. Instead of proving that the conviction of Schenk was correct, the Court's decision proved mainly that the justices agreed with current public thinking. That public mood proved fragile. More and more people grew uneasy about the increasing power of the government to take away individual freedoms. The American Civil Liberties Union was organized in 1920 by a group of people committed to preserving the guarantees set forth in the Bill of Rights.

Dangerous Tendency Test

Even Supreme Court justices who had ruled against Schenck saw the danger posed by too rigid a restriction on freedom of speech. Although Justices Holmes and Louis Brandeis upheld some convictions under the Sedition Act, they began to disagree with their colleagues in decisions that limited freedom of speech.

The break occurred shortly after

U.S. troops were sent to Russia during the Russian Revolution to fight against Russian natives. A group of Russian immigrant factory workers was distraught that weapons they made might be used against relatives still living in Russia.

the Schenck case. In 1918 five young Russian immigrants had protested the decision to send U.S. troops to Russia, where a revolution was taking place. They had printed thousands of pamphlets, which they had distributed by tossing the pamphlets from the open window of a building in New York City.

"Workers in the ammunition factories," the pamphlets said, "you are producing bullets, bayonets, cannon to murder not only the Germans, but also your dearest, best, who are in Russia fighting for freedom." One of the pamphlets ended with the words, "Workers, our reply to this barbaric intervention has to be a general strike."

The pamphlets were not intended to help Germany, with which United States was still at war. In fact, one pamphlet stated, "We hate and despise German militarism more than you do hypocritical tyrants." But a general strike of munitions workers at that time would have helped the Germans, regardless of the writers' intentions. Government officials prosecuted several of the people responsible for publishing the pamphlets.

When this case, *Abrams v. United States*, came before the Supreme Court, seven of the justices voted to uphold the conviction. In reaching their decision, they used a test known as the dangerous tendency test. The Court asked: Could the words of the speaker or writer start an action that could endanger public peace or national security? If so, they believed the government was justified in restricting such speech.

Clear and Present Danger Test

Holmes and Brandeis rejected the dangerous tendency test. They said it was not enough that the expression of ideas might lead to some danger; governments could use that as an excuse to stop any form of criticism. Instead, Holmes and Brandeis expanded the clear and present danger test that Holmes had first written about in the Schenck case. His test posed the questions: Does the expression of ideas present a serious threat to the security of the nation? Is that threat so great that immediate action would have to be taken to save the country?

In *Abrams v. United States*, Holmes argued that nobody could suppose that the publishing of a "silly leaflet by an unknown man" would present any immediate danger to the nation. Holmes added a further protection to individual expression. He said that expression of an idea could be considered as treason only if it was intended to hurt the United States. If the defendants had published their pamphlets in an effort to harm the United States, they would have been guilty of a crime under the Sedition Act of 1918. But the intention was to stop American intervention in Russia, and this was no crime, Holmes said.

In 1927, eight years after Holmes first proposed the clear and present danger test, Brandeis wrote an opinion that carried the test even further. Brandeis, with Holmes's agreement, said that even words which threaten to cause immediate danger cannot be restricted unless the danger feared is relatively serious.

Brandeis wrote:

Fear of serious injury cannot alone justify suppression of free speech and assembly. . . . No danger flowing from speech can be deemed clear and present, unless . . . [it] . . . is so imminent [close] that it may befall before there is opportunity for full discussion. If there be time to expose through discussion

These members of the 1925 Supreme Court were the first to rule that individual states could not restrict any of the rights guaranteed by the Constitution. Soon after their ruling, the Court began to hear more cases in which people claimed their constitutional rights had been violated.

the falsehood . . . to avert the evil by the process of education, the remedy to be applied is more speech, not enforced silence.

Justices Holmes and Brandeis raised a number of ideas about freedom of speech that were not immediately accepted by the other justices. Holmes received little support from fellow justices when he wrote:

. . . the best test of truth is the power of thought to get itself accepted in the competition of the market . . . I think that we should be eternally vigilant

against attempts to check the expression of opinions that we loathe . . .

But the ideas of Brandeis and Holmes gradually were accepted by new members of the Court and by the United States public.

Meanwhile, an opinion expressed in a 1925 Supreme Court ruling ensured that the Court would have plenty of chances to hear cases about freedom of speech. Before then, the Court had not ruled on cases that had to do with state laws. The justices had believed that the

45

Constitution assigned them to cover only cases involving the federal government actions. Since most of the controversial cases dealing with free speech involved state laws, the Court had seldom become involved in free speech cases.

But in 1925 the Supreme Court declared that the 14th Amendment to the Constitution protected people's right to free speech under state laws as well as federal laws. The 14th Amendment declared that no state could "deprive any person of life, liberty, or property, without due process of law…" In the Court's opinion, free speech was one of the liberties covered by the amendment. The Supreme Court then began to hear cases dealing with threats to freedom of expression that came from state governments, as well as the federal government. Ever since then, the Supreme Court has been on center stage in the debate about free speech.

Preferred Position

The issues of free speech during wartime were still being resolved when the United States entered World War II in 1941. As before, fear of foreign enemies sparked new laws limiting free speech. Even before the United States was officially involved in the war, restrictive legislation was passed. The 1940 Alien Registration Act, commonly known as the Smith Act, made it a crime to teach or encourage "subversive" ideas.

By this time, though, public opinion on freedom of speech had changed. A majority of the justices favored Holmes' clear and present danger test. Within a few years, more and more court decisions came out in favor of individual rights. The Court's stance was known as "preferred position." The term appeared

Justice William Douglas

World War II tanks head to a North African battlefront. During WWII, the Supreme Court began to overturn convictions of people who had criticized the war effort.

in a 1945 opinion issued by Justice Wiley Rutledge. Preferred position is the idea that First Amendment rights are so important to a free society that it is the duty of the Court to protect these freedoms even when they conflict with other rights.

Some people argued that this put the entire nation at risk, but Justice Hugo Black said the nation's founders realized the danger created by free speech. However, they felt the benefits were worth the risk, he said.

Justice William Douglas said government would have enough time to interfere when speeches prompted acts that could endanger the country during wartime.

The Court ruled that criticism of government policy during wartime is not necessarily treason. It said,

"A citizen may take actions which do aid and comfort the enemy— making a speech critical of the government . . . and a hundred other things which impair our cohesion and diminish our strength—but if there is no adherence to the enemy in this, if there is no intent to betray, there is no treason."

The more liberal stance of the Court during World War II limited the effects of the Smith Act. Only 89 persons were convicted under the Smith Act during the war, and only 29 of those served their sentences. Only one case, which was prosecuted under the Espionage Act of 1917, was argued before the Supreme Court. That conviction was overturned because justices felt it did not meet the criteria set up in the clear and present danger test.

In allowing greater individual liberty during World War II, the United States people discovered that the dangers of free speech were not as great as many had feared. The war effort suffered no harm from those who disagreed with government policies.

Serious Future Danger

Free speech versus national security has remained a delicate issue.

Just as the United States people have occasionally shifted their views on the subject, the Supreme Court has made adjustments.

During the early 1950s, the spread of communism throughout the world frightened many people in the United States. They viewed communism as an international conspiracy to destroy the United States government. Anyone who supported any of the ideas of communism was thought to be a dangerous traitor. As in the days of the Sedition Acts of 1798 and 1918, concerns about national security led people to limit speech they believed was dangerous.

The Supreme Court allowed the restrictions. Indeed, a majority of the Supreme Court justices echoed the fears of the public. They thought the "clear and present danger" test contained a major flaw: It did not offer enough protection against conspiracy to overthrow the government by force and violence. Conspiracies could gather strength over the years but be safe from the law because the danger was not yet immediate. By the time the danger was serious and immediate, it would be too late to save the country.

This led the Court to develop another test, in which it considered whether the words spoken or written were likely to cause serious danger in the future. By applying the serious future danger test, the Court permitted Congress and state legislatures to prohibit speech which favored the overthrow of the U.S. government by force. Speech that taught methods of overthrowing the government was also prohibited. The test soon proved to be imperfect. Under the serious future danger test, a simple speech in support of the ideals of communism could be —and was—considered a danger to the republic.

The Pendulum Swings Back

For a brief time, the Supreme Court upheld the convictions of people prosecuted for their communist beliefs. The most notable case was *Dennis v. United States* in 1951. In *Dennis* the Supreme Court upheld the convictions of 11 leaders of the Communist Party on a 6-to-2 vote. Within a few years, though, the Court resumed its support of preferred position for individuals. Two cases involving radically different points of view show the dramatic

Senator Joseph McCarthy, right, capitalized on a wave of fear over communism in the 1950s by bringing people he suspected of communist activity before official committee hearings.

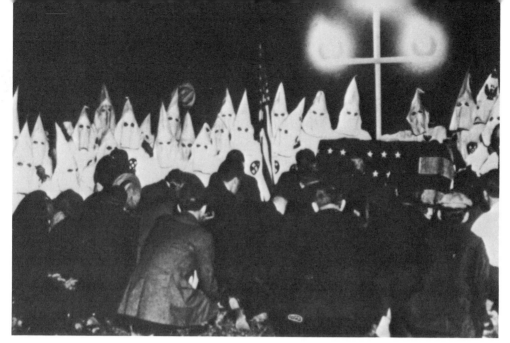

The Supreme Court has ruled that even speech that most people find deplorable, such as the racist rhetoric voiced by the Ku Klux Klan, is protected by the First Amendment.

shift that occurred between 1919 and the 1970s.

In 1969 the Supreme Court listened to arguments in the case of *Brandenburg v. Ohio.* Clarence Brandenburg was a member of a white superiority group, the Ku Klux Klan. In 1964 he had appeared on television denouncing certain minority groups. He stated that "niggers should be returned to Africa and the Jews should be returned to Israel." He also suggested that if the government did not stand up for the "rights" of the white race, they (the Ku Klux Klan) "might have to take revenge." Prosecutors for the state of Ohio

had won a conviction against Brandenburg for inciting violence.

The Supreme Court, however, reversed the decision. Regardless of how repulsive an idea was, the Court ruled, states may not punish a person for expressing his or her belief in it. Justice William Douglas said that even suggesting the use of force is permitted under the Constitution—if the suggestion does not lead to immediate lawless action. *Brandenburg* reminded people that the purpose of the Court is not to judge whether an idea is right, but only whether the expression of it is legal.

About the same time that the

The country's feelings about Vietnam War protests were reflected in court decisions of the 1970s. Overall, the courts upheld people's freedom to say anything they felt about the war.

Brandenburg decision was made, the case of Dr. Benjamin Spock came before the First United States Circuit Court of Appeals. Spock was one of a group of protesters convicted of interfering with the draft and the government's military efforts during the Vietnam War. Although the case did not reach the Supreme Court, the appeal court's verdict was in line with the standards set by the Supreme Court. Spock's conviction was overturned on a unanimous opinion of the court. In its decision, the court stated that vigorous criticism of the draft and of the Vietnam War was free speech protected by the First Amendment. Although the appeals court justices agreed that Spock's intent was to hinder the war effort, they said there was no evidence of a criminal conspiracy.

These were the same arguments that had been used in the Schenck case 50 years earlier. Schenck had taken nearly the same actions as

Although police clashed with Vietnam War demonstrators, the courts rarely found the demonstrators guilty of sedition. The people arrested at these demonstrations were more likely to be charged with disorderly conduct.

Spock had, yet he had been convicted for breaking the law. By 1970 Spock's actions were considered to be protected by the First Amendment.

History has shown that interpretations of the law can change drastically. What will happen if a case similar to Spock's and Schenck's occurs 30 years from now? The debate over free speech certainly will continue.

Balancing One Right Against Another

Free speech does not concern only individual rights and national security. Society has not yet come up with ways to balance the rights of two individuals or groups. A prime example is a march that the American Nazi Party proposed in 1977. First a mostly-black group had marched into the all-white Chicago suburb of Cicero, Illinois, to demonstrate for civil rights. Next the Nazis requested permission to march in front of the Skokie, Illinois, village hall dressed in full Nazi uniforms. Skokie is a city with a mostly Jewish population. During World War II, German Nazis had killed millions of Jewish people and confined millions more to concentration camps. The concentration camps had been horrible

Should a group that aligns itself with the WWII-era Nazis of Germany be allowed to march down a street populated by a large number of Jewish people?

Prisoners of a German concentration camp celebrate their coming release toward the end of World War II. Millions of Jewish people were killed in the camps and others were confined and subject to cruel treatment. Later, many of the camp survivors immigrated to the United States.

places, and survivors of the camps were haunted by the memories of the cruel treatment they received. Several thousand survivors of the camps lived in Skokie.

Skokie's citizens were insulted by the American Nazi Party's plans to march in their city, and they tried to ban the march. The courts upheld the right of the Nazis to march in Skokie, but public opinion was solidly against it. The group eventually canceled the march.

Another unresolved issue between the rights of two groups involves speakers and hecklers. Should heckling be banned because it denies the person making the speech the right to express an opinion? Or does that infringe upon the right of the heckler to express his or her opinion?

There is certainly no way that everyone in a nation of more than 200 million people can agree on responsible and necessary limits to free speech. Former Supreme Court Justice Robert Jackson made a strong case for restricting free speech in 1950 when he said, "If the Court does not temper its doctrinaire logic with a little practical wisdom, it will convert the constitutional Bill of Rights into a suicide pact." Many people agreed with him. Yet the reluctance of the country's founders to make government too powerful has also been proven to be well grounded. For instance, in the 1960s, some government agencies began to consider any kind of disagreement with the government as treason. Thousands of U.S. citizens were illegally watched, followed, photographed, and taped simply because they held opinions that were different from those held by the government administration. Such actions make many people wary of allowing the government to restrict free speech. The *New York Times* echoed words written long ago by John Milton when it editorialized that the question is whether you believe in freedom or fear it.

While the uncertainty surrounding free speech may be unsettling, many people believe the ongoing debate is good. Scholars have argued that it is this continuing, lively debate that has helped the United States Constitution survive longer than any other written constitution in the world. Each of us needs to be a part of that debate to help ensure that the flow of ideas and beliefs is as free as we would like.

Are people within their rights to use equipment that lets their voices be heard further away?

5
You Make the Decision

This actual case was argued before the Supreme Court in 1951. How would you decide the case?

Facts of the Case

A university student named Irving Feiner stood on top of a box on a street corner in Syracuse, New York, and began to make a speech. His words, which were carried over a loudspeaker mounted on a car, attracted an audience of about 75 listeners. They crowded the sidewalk so much that people wishing to walk past had to pass on the street.

During his speech, Feiner called President Harry Truman a "bum" and the American Legion a "Nazi Gestapo." He accused the mayor of

Was Feiner within his rights to call President Harry Truman a bum?

Syracuse, whom he called a "champagne-sipping bum," of not speaking for black people. But the trouble really started when Feiner said: "The Negroes don't have equal rights; they should rise up in arms and fight for them." That was too much for one man, who said that if police did not get Feiner off the stand, he would do so himself.

Two policemen on the scene said there was an angry muttering throughout the crowd, and some pushing was taking place. They were afraid a riot would break out. Twice they told Feiner to stop speaking, but the student refused. Finally he was arrested.

Feiner's case was first heard in a New York trial court. The trial judge ruled that the police were justified in arresting Feiner to prevent a "breach of the peace" and found Feiner guilty of disorderly conduct.

Convinced that his constitutional right to free speech had been violated, Feiner appealed his case to the New York Court of Appeals. When that court upheld the conviction, Feiner took his case to the New York State Supreme Court and finally to the United States Supreme Court.

Did Feiner have the right to make the speech and to denounce President Truman, the mayor of Syracuse, and the American Legion? Was he within his rights to use loud-speaking equipment? Was his constitutional right to free speech violated by the police? How would you rule in this case?

The Verdict

A majority of the Supreme Court justices voted to uphold the judgment of the lower courts. Chief Justice Fred Vinson explained that Feiner was not convicted for anything he said in the speech. It was his constitutional right to express his opinions about the president, mayor, and American Legion. He was also within his rights to use loud-speaking equipment. According to Vinson, Feiner did not break the law until the expression of his views caused the danger of a riot. The police were correct in trying to prevent that public disturbance, asking him to stop, and arresting him when he continued to speak.

In his majority opinion, Vinson said:

> (The courts) found that the officers in making the arrest were motivated solely by a proper concern for the preservation of order and protection of the general welfare, and that there

Chief Justice Fred Vinson said the police can arrest a person if his or her speech threatens public safety.

...When clear and present danger of riot, disorder, interference with traffic upon the public streets, or other immediate threat to public safety, peace, or order appears, the power of the State to prevent or punish is obvious.

...ordinary murmurings and objections of a hostile audience cannot be allowed to silence a speaker, and we are also mindful of the possible danger of giving overzealous police officials complete discretion to break up otherwise lawful public meetings. But we are not faced here with such a situation. It is one thing to say that the police cannot be used [to suppress] unpopular views, and another to say that, when as here the speaker passes the bounds of argument or persuasion and [tries to cause a] riot, they are powerless to prevent a breach of peace...

In his dissenting opinion, Justice Black said:

...The police of course have power to prevent breaches of the peace. But if, in the name of preserving order, they ever can interfere with a lawful public speaker, they first must make all reasonable efforts to protect him.... According to the officers' testimony, the

was no evidence which could lend color to a claim that the acts of the police were a cover for suppression of [his] views and opinions. [Feiner] was thus neither arrested nor convicted for the making or the content of his speech. Rather it was the reaction which it actually engendered.

Free speech that poses no danger to public safety, such as a peaceful labor rally, is allowed.

crowd was restless but there is no showing of any attempt to quiet it; pedestrians were forced to walk into the street, but there was no effort to clear a path on the sidewalk; one person threatened to assault [Feiner] but the officers did nothing to discourage this when even a word might have sufficed. Their duty was to protect [Feiner's] right to talk, even to the extent of arresting the man who threatened to interfere . . .

Justice Douglas, joined by Justice Sherman Minton, wrote a separate dissenting opinion, in which he said:

A speaker may not, of course, incite a riot any more than he may incite a breach of the peace by the use of "fighting words" . . . But this record shows no such extremes. It shows an unsympathetic audience and the threat of one man to haul the speaker from the stage. It is against that kind of threat that speakers need police protection. If they do not receive it and instead the police throw their weight on the side of those who would break up the meetings, the police become the new censors of speech. . . .

Who was right?

6
Your Right to Free Speech

Specific rules about freedom of speech are not always easy to figure out. The Supreme Court, lawmakers, and the public will always debate how much free speech can be allowed before the nation's security is threatened. Generally, the courts have upheld the principle of free speech, even when popular opinion was against it.

Supreme Court interpretations have given us some general guidelines for free speech.

What You Can Do Under Your Right to Free Speech

1. You may stand on a street corner and make a speech giving your views on religion, government, law, or any other subject. However, if the crowd that gathers around you spills out into the streets, stopping traffic or causing danger of accidents, the police may ask you to move.

2. You are free to pass out pamphlets in public places, such as street corners or parks. You do not need a permit for this so long as your material is an expression of your views and not an advertisement for a commercial product or project.

3. You may make a speech in a public park, but you may be required to get a license or permit to do so. The license may be denied because of concerns over traffic, normal use of the park, and public safety. It cannot be refused because of anything you plan to say in your speech.

4. You may ring doorbells and ask people to listen to your views on religion or politics. You may also leave pamphlets inside of their doors, but not in their mailboxes. A resident who does not want people coming to the door to express their opinions must post a sign that contains this information.

5. You may organize a group to walk through the streets, carrying protest signs, speaking, singing, or chanting.

You may be required to get a parade license, however. The license may be denied if there are concerns about traffic and safety. The license may not be denied because officials do not like the ideas you plan to express.

6. You may express ideas that you know the audience will not like. If the audience becomes angry and threatens you, the police will usually protect your right to speak and will attempt to keep order among the

Judges on the 1990 Supreme Court are (seated, left to right) Thurgood Marshall, William Brennan, Jr., Chief Justice William H. Rehnquist, Byron R. White, Harry A. Blackmun, (standing) Antonin Scalia, John Paul Stevens, Sandra Day O'Connor, and Anthony M. Kennedy.

People will usually be allowed to march in the streets of a city, as Martin Luther King (at left in front row) and these civil rights marchers did in Washington, D.C., during 1963. But they may have to apply for a parade license. Such an application may be denied if officials believe the parade will create undue traffic problems.

audience. If the audience gets out of control, however, you will be asked to stop speaking and may be punished if you do not stop.

7. You can make a speech or pass out pamphlets which attempt to show that communism, socialism, fascism, or any other form of government is better than democracy. There is no danger of arrest unless you urge the overthrow of the United States government by force and violence.

8. You may publicly criticize people holding public office and candidates for public office unless it is obvious that you are lying in an effort to hurt them.

What You Cannot Do Under Your Right to Free Speech

1. You cannot make a speech or hand out printed materials in a privately owned place such as a restaurant, hotel, department store, or theater lobby unless you have the permission of the property manager.

2. You cannot speak in a park or organize a march if you have been denied a license, even if you think the license was denied illegally. You may seek help from the courts,

however, if you believe the license was improperly denied.

3. According to a 1988 Supreme Court ruling, you may not picket a private home if there is a local ordinance that prohibits you from doing so.

4. You cannot say or write false things about a person outside of public office that will damage that person's reputation, business life, or personal life. If the words are spoken, the crime is slander. If the words are written, the crime is libel.

5. Although you can protest against the draft and United States participation in a war, you can be arrested if you teach people how to use illegal methods to keep them from being drafted.

6. You cannot use "fighting words" in a speech you are making. That is, you cannot say such insulting things about a member of the audience that a fight is likely to break out as a result. This limitation is not used as widely as it used to be, however.

7. In communities that have "group libel" laws, you may not make speeches or pass out pamphlets attacking or ridiculing a particular race, religion, or organization if such speech is likely to provoke violence.

8. In speaking, or in printed materials, you cannot urge people to commit a crime if there is a reasonable chance that your efforts will get them to do so. For example, you can make a speech in which you criticize the poor garbage collection in your city, but you might get arrested if you told your audience to throw garbage on the mayor's lawn.

Conclusion

The First Amendment protects the right of all U.S. citizens to express their thoughts. Through the years, however, officials have sought to balance the right to free speech with other rights protected by constitutional amendments. Continued efforts to balance these sometimes conflicting rights will ensure a lively debate on the right to free speech for years to come.

The debate over free speech will continue for years as government officials and the courts seek a balance between individual rights and public safety.

Appendix

The Bill of Rights

The Bill of Rights was added to the Constitution of the United States in 1791, after it was ratified, or approved, by the states of New Jersey, Maryland, North Carolina, South Carolina, New Hampshire, Delaware, New York, Pennsylvania, Rhode Island, Vermont, and Virginia. The first 10 amendments to the Constitution, called articles, make up the Bill of Rights.

Article I

Congress shall make no law respecting an establishment of religion, or prohibiting the free exercise thereof; or abridging the freedom of speech, or of the press; or the right of the people peaceably to assemble, and to petition the Government for a redress of grievances.

Article II

A well regulated Militia, being necessary to the security of a free State, the right of the people to keep and bear Arms, shall not be infringed.

Article III

No Soldier shall, in time of peace be quartered in any house, without the consent of the Owner, nor in time of war, but in a manner prescribed by law.

Article IV

The right of the people to be secure in their persons, houses, papers and effects, against unreasonable searches and seizures, shall not be violated, and no Warrants shall issue, but upon probable cause, supported by Oath or affirmation, and particularly describing the place to be searched, and the persons or things to be seized.

Article V

No person shall be held to answer for a capital, or otherwise infamous crime, unless on a presentment of indictment of a Grand Jury, except in cases arising in the land or naval forces, or in the Militia, when in actual service in time of War or public danger; nor shall any person be subject for the same offence to be twice put in jeopardy of life or limb; nor shall be compelled in any criminal case to be a witness against himself, nor be deprived of life, liberty, or property, without due process of law; nor shall private property be taken for public use without just compensation.

Article VI

In all criminal prosecutions the accused shall enjoy the right to a speedy and public trial, by an impartial jury of the State and district wherein the crime shall have been committed, which district shall have been previously ascertained by law, and to be informed of the nature and cause of the accusation; to be confronted with the witness against him; to have compulsory process for obtaining Witnesses in his favor, and to have the assistance of counsel for his defense.

Article VII

In Suits at common law, where the value in controversy shall exceed twenty dollars, the right of trial by jury shall be preserved, and no fact tried by a jury, shall be otherwise reexamined in any Court of the United States, than according to the rules of the common law.

Article VIII

Excessive bail shall not be required, nor excessive fines imposed, nor cruel and unusual punishments inflicted.

Article IX

The enumeration in the Constitution, of certain rights, shall not be construed to deny or disparage others retained by the people.

Article X

The powers not delegated to the United States by the Constitution, nor prohibited by it to the States, are reserved to the States respectively, or to the people.

For Further Reading

Bollinger, Lee C. *The Tolerant Society: Freedom of Speech and Extremist Speech in America.* New York: Oxford University Press, 1986.

Cox, Archibald. *Freedom of Expression.* Cambridge, Massachusetts: Harvard University Press, 1981.

Downs, Donald A. *Nazis in Skokie: Freedom, Community, and the First Amendment.* Notre Dame, Indiana: University of Notre Dame Press, 1985.

Fincher, E.B. *The Bill of Rights.* New York: Franklin Watts, Inc., 1978.

Hentoff, Nat. *The First Freedom: The Tumultuous History of Free Speech in America.* New York: Delacorte Press, 1980.

Kalven, Harry, Jr. *A Worthy Tradition: Freedom of Speech in America.* New York: Harper & Row, Publishers, 1988.

Kleinknecht, C. Fred. *Anchor of Liberty.* Washington, D.C.: The Supreme Council, 33° Ancient and Accepted Scottish Rite of Freemasonry of the Southern Jurisdiction of the United States of America, 1987.

Kohn, Bernice. *The Spirit of the Letter: The Struggle for Rights in America.* New York: The Viking Press, 1974.

Lieberman, Jethro. *Free Speech, Free Press, and the Law.* New York: Lothrop, Lee & Shepard, 1980.

Morris, Richard B. *The American Revolution.* Minneapolis, Minnesota: Lerner Publications Co., 1985.

——. *The Constitution.* Minneapolis, Minnesota: Lerner Publications Co., 1985.

——. *The Founding of the Republic.* Minneapolis, Minnesota: Lerner Publications Co., 1985.

Important Words

The terms listed below are defined on the indicated page.

censorship, 18
libel, 29
licenses, 18
majority opinion, 38

minority opinion, 38
Parliament, 16
public opinion, 11
seditious libel, 22

slander, 22
treason, 16
values, 14

Index

Acknowledgments

The photographs and illustrations in this book are reproduced through the courtesy of: David Rae Morris, p. 2; Close-Up Foundation/Renee Bouchard, pp. 6, 65; The Library of Congress, pp. 8, 9, 11, 19, 30, 31, 36, 38, 39, 40, 42, 45, 50, 53, 59, 71; National Abortion Rights Action League, p. 12; Independent Picture Service, pp. 14, 17; Musées Nationaux, Paris, p. 15; Trustees of the British Museum, p. 16; New York Public Library/Astor, Lenox and Tilden Foundations, p. 20 (left); Yale University, p. 20 (right); New York Public Library, p. 21; The Metropolitan Museum of Art, Gift of John S. Kennedy, 1897, p. 22; The Virginia Museum of Fine Arts, Gift of Colonel and Mrs. Edgar W. Garbisch, 1950, p. 24; Museum of Fine Arts, Boston, p. 26 (left); Dictionary of American Portraits, p. 26 (right); National Gallery of Art, Washington, D.C., p. 27 (left); Independence National Historical Park Collection, p. 27 (right); Supreme Court Historical Society, pp. 29, 41; National Archives, pp. 32, 33, 35, 43, 46, 47, 54, 56, 63; U.S. Senate Historical Office, p. 49; Minneapolis Tribune, p. 51; United Press International, p. 52; U.S. Army, Harry S. Truman Library, p. 57; Lori Waselchuk, p. 60; and Asman Photo, p. 62.

Read more about the United
States political system in
these Lerner books:

Presidential Campaign
by Thomas R. Raber

Election Night
by Thomas R. Raber

Freedom of the Press
by J. Edward Evans

Freedom of Religion
by J. Edward Evans